care·giv·er
defined

Words that honor the work of the caregiver

Michael Fortuna

illustrations by Peg Lee

SAVERIO PRESS

Saverio Press
www.saveriopress.com

Bulk Ordering Information:

Special discounts are available on quantity purchases by corporations, associations and others. For details, email the publisher at **bulk@saveriopress.com**.

ISBN 978-0-9988376-0-4

First Edition

Definitions of words in this book are either statements of widely known facts, or simple expressions of the author based on a particular word's use in each accompanying paragraph. This book is not a reference or educational work, and does not attempt to provide the concise and multiple meanings of words found in professional reference volumes.

SAVERIO PRESS
www.saveriopress.com

For Peter

What are brothers for?

Acknowledgements

First, I would like to offer my gratitude to my friend and illustrator, Peg Lee, who brought the pages of this book to life through her beautiful illustrations.

I would like to thank my wife, Kathleen, and my family for all their support, and call special attention to my sister, Anne, whose unwavering care of our parents in their elder years was further inspiration to write this book. I would also like to acknowledge Richard Emerson, long-time personal mentor, critic and cheerleader, Mia McNiece, for her help and support, as well as Maura Atkinson Butler who provided her copy-editing skills to this book.

Finally, I would like to thank all of the caregivers and their families who read this book while it was still in progress. What was even more gratifying than their positive feedback was the surprise unveiling of their own personal vocabularies connected to caregiving. A number of them offered unsolicited and heartfelt words that represented their own personal experiences, reassuring me that I had found a common lexicon capable of articulating some of the many, deep-seated emotions that caregivers share.

Introduction

Whether limited to being a driver for an occasional doctor's appointment or dedicated to intense long-term care, caregivers, in many respects, are some of the hardest working and most generous people in the world. And even while there are millions of individuals providing care at any given time, many unfortunately still feel isolated and alone in their endeavors. They shouldn't.

This simple book, inspired by my own imperfect bouts with caregiving, is meant to honor caregivers, to define them through nouns, verbs and adjectives that connect in some way to the hard work they do as well as the wide range of emotions that accompany their efforts. While there are more comprehensive volumes that serve caregivers in expanded and in-depth ways, this book merely strives to make them aware that their challenges are both recognized and heartily supported. In that respect, think of it as a casserole for caregivers, an awkward but sincere gift left on the doorstep that will make them feel more understood and validated. This book is not a cure-all, or even a cure at all for the difficulties of serving someone in need. It's just a way to say "great job, keep going, thank you!"

My hope is that this book finds its way into the hands of caregivers and it helps them feel acknowledged, appreciated and most of all, good about themselves. And I hope it will be read by the families and friends of caregivers, making them more aware of just how special caregiving is.

In the end, compassion and empathy are two of humanity's greatest traits, and no one sets a more stellar example of those virtues in action than caregivers. Their blood, sweat and tears make the world a more humane place for everyone. And there is great promise in that.

care·giv·er

noun

A person who helps another in need.

con·fi·dence

noun

The trait of feeling sure or certain.

*One of the most difficult aspects of caring for another is trying to find the **confidence** in yourself that will allow you to serve their needs. You have no previous experience on which to lean, no instruction book to go by, and no one to whom you can turn. But what you do have is something even more valuable – the loving clarity of purpose that blesses your efforts, and in the process, works its wonders on the person who so depends on you.*

dig·ni·ty

noun

The condition of being deserving of esteem or regard.

At the very core of your efforts is your defense of human **dignity**. *You may be powerless against the ravages of old age and disease, but you perform miracles of the spirit. With encouraging words, consoling hands, and most of all with the simple act of your very presence. Your standing by someone in need is a declaration that one, single life matters. Not just to you. But to the entire world.*

mem·o·ry

noun

The capacity of recognizing previous thoughts
or experiences.

*The gift of **memory** is most precious when you become the memory for another. When you become the GPS for the teakettle, the finder of socks in a drawer, and the keeper of pills as if they were your own. Memory becomes sacred when you remember what they cannot. And that simple act of love will be something for which you will be forever remembered.*

ap·point·ed

verb

Assigned or designated.

How did you get this job? Did you draw the short straw? Call heads instead of tails? Lose at Rock-Paper-Scissors? Regardless, you have been **appointed** *"The Caregiver." Unfairly perhaps, you hold another life in your hands. And while you may not have a choice in the task, you do in your response to it. Try to find it within yourself to make it a beautiful one.*

choc·o·late

noun

A confection made from roasted cacao seeds.

In between the difficult hours of caregiving, you need to find some **chocolate***, something sweet to take your mind off of the work you do. That can be reading a few tasty pages of your favorite novel, watching a morsel of a television show, or even recalling a leftover memory from some treasured moment in your past. While you will never shirk responsibility, make sure there is something delectable to momentarily turn to, so that in some small way you can renew yourself, and be ready again to take on the challenge.*

ar·chi·vist

noun

A keeper of archives or records.

As a caregiver, a life is spread before you. Through the unbreakable trust created by your care, you hear things — whispers from them that astound. Some make you laugh, others make you cry or cringe. But it is a special honor to be invited into the inner sanctum of another. You have the opportunity to be the **archivist** *for another human being. And whether you keep it to yourself or share it within your personal community, remember that it is a great privilege to record a life lived, to be gifted with such secrets of the human heart.*

pan

noun

A metal or earthenware container for domestic use.

*You are caught in the middle of the battle, "Bedpan vs. Pot and **Pan**." On one side is that person in need, hungry for your help. On the other is that little voice inside telling you that you are not doing enough for your family. So, to whom do you listen? Listen to neither. Just do what you can for both sides, and remember to wash your hands in between.*

e·mo·ji

noun

A small icon or symbol used to express
emotions in text messages.

*Which **emoji** will you be today? If it's a bad day, you might be the face that grits its teeth at the grunt work of caregiving. If it's a day originally planned for yourself and your own needs, then you might be the emoji with tears of self-pity running down its face, or even the one hiding its true feelings behind a pair of sunglasses. Every day of caregiving can be difficult, sometimes supremely so. But it's also an invitation to choose. In your inventory of emojis, find one that says "I got this" – an emoji that can face the day with determination and just a hint of delight at being blessed with the opportunity to help another.*

tears

noun

Drops of saline fluid diffused between the eyes and the eyelids.

Tears *are the Swiss army knives of caregiving, coming in handy for any number of emotional needs. When all of a sudden all is beautiful, tears form your fountain of joy. When the fire of a hard day's care begins to rage, they hose it down, almost to a smolder. And when your mind overflows with all you need to do, the stress-turned-to-tears seeps under the lids of your eyes, relieving you, if only just for a moment. In caregiving, tears are good. Make use of them, as they are the ultimate coping mechanism – nature's way of irrigating an arid human soul.*

sac·ri·fice

verb

To relinquish something in favor of something more important.

While so many in the world hold their arms stiffly by their sides when asked to volunteer, the outstretched arm of the caregiver stands high and unselfishly in the air. You're not afraid to share the life needs of another. And your willingness to **sacrifice** *is beyond reproach. You're willing to put your own dreams aside and face the reality before you. And you would trade almost anything just to make them whole and healthy again. Regardless of the return, you sacrifice one hundred percent of yourself. And while you may not realize it, there are many, many people who are thankful that you raised your hand.*

ab·sent

adjective

Being away from a place, not in attendance.

Absent *is something you may feel every day. Caregiving can be so enormous that it takes you away from your family, your friends, and even from yourself. And while absence is painful on everyone, the work that you do sets a Mother Teresa-size example for those in your life who will be called to care in the future. You can take comfort in being a catalyst for such a loving effort.*

pa·tience

noun

The act of calmly waiting for something.

Patience, *like batteries, is not included in your caregiving package. It's something you need to find on your own. And that takes an unselfishness of time, a willingness to lose part of your day, part of your life, in the care of another. And while you may give up part of your own valuable time, there is an upside. Because once you have patience it will never go away, allowing you to better appreciate family, friends and to bask in the moment of just being alive and well.*

black·board

noun

A slate board on which writing can be done with chalk.

When the slate of someone's mind is wiped clean by disease, you get out the chalk and fill the **blackboard** again. You will not allow a life so full to be ticketed as one so empty. So, you rebuild it for them day by day, every day. And even if they can't comprehend your glowing biography you remain undaunted, faithfully believing that deep inside their silence is a soul smiling with affection as you recite the rich details of their life.

in·stinc·tive

adjective

Having an innate or automatic understanding.

*If you learn by doing, then you learn even more by doing it over and over again. As challenging as caregiving can be, it does make you powerfully **instinctive**. You become intimate with the needs of another, so close to them that in an uncanny way, you can anticipate when they will arise. But what makes your instinctiveness truly remarkable is that you never accept as gospel what you hear from others concerning your care. You run it by your own heart and soul first. And that makes for a caregiver of the finest kind.*

hu·mor

noun

The ability to appreciate comical or absurd
elements in a situation.

*You know you have reached the highest form of care-giving when you can find **humor** in the work you do. The ability to laugh at the turmoil in your life, at those involved in it, and especially at yourself. When days are darkest, just imagine yourself as a rodeo clown in a barrel, coaxing the bull to charge you instead of the person for whom you care. Wave your arms. Roar with laughter. Show the bull you're up to the task.*

un·self·ish

adjective

Displaying more consideration for the welfare
of others than one's own.

Unselfish *is how everyone but you, describes you. That's why you need to be more generous with yourself. Pack away your guilt for another day. Be patient with your impatience. Take "not good enough" and file it under "done." You are the best caregiver you can be. And that is the epitome of unselfish.*

guilt·y

adjective

Culpable for a fault, error or wrongdoing.

*If you allow it, you will always be found **guilty** in the courtroom inside your mind. Guilty of never doing enough. Guilty of doing it with less than the perfect smile. Guilty of doing your good works, only out of guilt. Guilt is always there to point its finger of accusation. Pay no attention. Because in the higher court of human kindness, many witnesses will come forward on your behalf, stating not only your innocence, but also praising your generosity and sense of justice to those in need.*

heart

noun

A muscular organ that pumps and circulates blood in a body.

The caregiver's **heart** *enlarges through its labors of love, making it stronger than you ever thought possible. Making it able to push a person uphill. To hold a broken body tightly. And able to maintain its rhythm even in the most arrhythmic, stressful moments. The caregiver's heart is the humble heart of an unlikely hero, giving its all to the needs of another, with never a thought to its own mortality.*

watch·dog

noun

A person that guards and protects another from potential danger and harm.

You are no Chihuahua trembling in the corner, nor some purse puppy carried around from mall to mall, yipping at those less endowed. No – you have found your voice and it is a strong one. You have found your stance and it is a powerful one. You are a **watchdog** *facing the large and fierce monster of caregiving. And while sometimes you may be tempted to cower, you somehow find it within yourself to growl at all obstacles, to unequivocally proclaim your loyalty to the needs of another.*

trans·form

verb

To change, typically in a dramatic manner.

One of the most beautiful benefits of caregiving is its ability to **transform** *you and the way you view the world. Caregiving changes you. It forces you to look at each sunrise in a different way. Makes you more aware of the rhythm of your own breathing. And reminds you just how fragile and surprising life can be. Caregiving is hard, close-to-the-bone work. But it also opens up a door to a sense of awareness you may have never experienced. All you have to do is give yourself permission to walk through, and you will be transformed.*

wait

verb

To remain ready for something to occur.

*You **wait** for hours in the doctor's office. In line at the pharmacy. On hold with the insurance company. All for the benefit of another. And while your mind may come up with millions of better ways to spend your time, remember that there is nothing more beatific or generous than giving so much of your time to someone who may have little quality time left.*

em·pa·thy

noun

The capacity to experience how another person feels.

*Food, clothing, shelter, **empathy**. When providing care, there is nothing more essential than empathy, one of the most basic human necessities and the very core of the compassionate caregiver. Empathy is the constant flow of reassurance from you that you know how they feel, and in some small way that acknowledgement makes them feel better and more secure. Empathy is you at your most humanly powerful, when all that matters is all that matters. And by your very willingness to take on the life of another, you too become one of life's necessities – food, clothing, shelter, you.*

jan·i·tor

noun

An individual who is a custodian or cleaner
of a building.

*You are like an angelic **janitor** that has come down from the basement of heaven to clean up the halls of the ill and aged. Quietly, humbly, you do your job, expecting nothing in return. And while there may be many janitorial moments of feeling you're at the low end in the hierarchy of human accomplishments, what you do is most holy. Sweep your halls with that as your joy, your satisfaction.*

oomph

noun

Zest, zip or enthusiasm.

Caregiving is not some weighty oath made in candlelight. It's an **oomph!** *It's finding the energy to get up every morning and take on the multitasking world that you've been handed. It's your willingness to balance family, friends and yourself with someone who desperately needs your time. Somehow, you find a way to satisfy each, to keep them all in your loop. And even the most solemn oath can't do that. That of course, takes oomph!*

re·sent·ment

noun

A feeling of indignation because of perceived unfairness.

Resentment *is the evil twin of Compassion, the two unable to be separated in the world of caregiving. And while your heart would like to deny its very existence, that most commonplace human emotion is there in the shadows waiting for you. So just as you acknowledge your compassion, you also need to honor your resentment. Scream in the mirror. Pound your fist. Slam the door. Kick your tires. By dealing with it, you diffuse it. And once you're empty of resentment, you will be calm and maybe even happy, ready to begin again.*

glue

noun

A substance with adhesive qualities.

When someone's life begins to come undone, you are the **glue** *that holds it together. When their spirit breaks, you repair it with a generous dab of compassion. And on those days when they're just falling apart, you somehow find a way to paste them back together again. You are the miracle glue that works wonders on those who need it most — its secret ingredient being the special stickiness of your unlimited love and sincerity.*

worm

noun

A slender small invertebrate animal with
no appendages or limbs.

You are now at the other end of the **worm**. *Once the baby robin. Now the parent robin to your own aging parents. Now is your time to provide food, shelter and care to those who did the same for you. To be the protector against all prey. In the endless recycling of human roles, you now have an opportunity not to pay back, but to say thank you through your care of those who hold a unique place in your life. They brought you into this world, and now you will help them leave it with grace and dignity.*

cour·age

noun

The capacity to face something difficult.

While most consider **courage** *to be something lionhearted, the caregiver knows better – you know that courage is often nothing more than fear with a positive attitude. You know that your willingness alone allows you to be a makeshift physician, nurse, nutritionist or even a psychologist or psychiatrist. Even better, you do so without giving it a second thought, without apologies. And that's a form of courage of a whole different kind.*

wine

noun

The fermented juice of grapes.

God made grapes with the caregiver in mind. He knew they would come in handy at the end of a difficult day, one fermented through the grind of the hard work you do. A glass of **wine** *can do wonders. It lets you exhale, unwind, and it can even wash away some of your unnecessary guilt. So, make your choice – red or white. And of course, let your toast include your promise to be bright-eyed and bushy-tailed in your next day of care. As the saying goes, care-give responsibly.*

ace

noun

A playing card containing only one image.

*You are the **ace** up humanity's sleeve. While mankind is in danger of losing its identity as it becomes more me-first, your simple good works offset the downfall. Everything you do in your care of another helps humanity rebuild itself, one good work at a time. So never feel that what you're doing is in vain. Not only are you ministering to someone in need, but in the process, you are also saving humanity from itself by making up for the shortcomings of others, as well as cutting a path of compassion for others to follow.*

box·ing

verb

To fight using only one's fists.

Even while you care for another, you must fight your own demons. When **boxing** *with your guilt, give a hard left to its body. Hurl an uppercut to the jaw of your resentment. And a knockout punch to the belly of your self-pity. Your demons only want you to take your eyes off the prize – the simple goodness and generosity of your care. Fight to do otherwise.*

hand·ker·chief

noun

A square of linen, cotton or other fabric for wiping eyes, nose or face.

Caregiving at its most human is a shared **handkerchief**, *one passed back and forth between the two of you, with never a thought to the occasional germ. That simple piece of fabric plays such a large and varied role – wiping mouths, drying tears, fixing the runny nose. It is the daily gauze of the caregiver, first aid for anything that gets in the way of human dignity, something you are determined to protect, and why it's wise to pack a clean handkerchief every day.*

sig·nif·i·cance

noun

Something of importance or consequence.

A hand held. A face washed. A meal prepared. Small acts of great **significance**, *true hallmarks of the caregiver. Even as the quiet work you do often goes unnoticed, it roots its way throughout the world. Because everything you do for another brings our planet closer together, and makes it a more humane place for all. In the end, the unselfish acts you perform, however small, provide a much-needed sense of gravitas to daily living, giving each day meaning far beyond the shallow promises of wealth, position or fame.*

cheer·lead·er

noun

Someone who supports and encourages
through cheering.

Even in the face of a certain and lopsided loss, you remain an enthusiastic **cheerleader**. *Not with pom-poms, cartwheels and handstands, but with the gentle empathy and understanding of someone who truly cares not only about the eventual outcome, but also about the day-to-day battle taking place on the human field before you. For you, giving up is never an option. And that itself is a victory of the moral kind.*

pol·li·na·tor

noun

A bee or insect that collects and transfers
pollen, one who pollinates.

Sometimes it's easy to dismiss your countless hours of care as just time lost in your own life, nothing more than insignificant days, months and sometimes even years. But that's not the truth. You not only do the heavy lifting but you, above all, are a **pollinator**, *transferring the good works you do into the hearts of others. While caregiving lives in the moment of need, the good deeds themselves find their way to others who will eventually blossom in their own caregiving – all because of you. And the significance of that certainly makes up for any lost time.*

sit

verb

To watch over someone, to keep vigil.

*Sometimes, the most transformative form of caregiving is to just **sit** with them in silence. You don't have to say anything for your love to be heard. And each stroke and squeeze of your hand on theirs speaks of compassion in the sign language of caregivers. Just sitting there is the ultimate commitment to caregiving – a simple physical act that embodies your promise to do whatever necessary.*

ad·mi·ra·tion

noun

Appreciation, respect or regard.

You don't seek acknowledgement or honor. You do what you do out of love and responsibility. Perhaps that's why others around you are speechless about your good works. They say nothing because they're unsure they could make the same sacrifices as you. But take heart in knowing that their silence shines with **admiration** *for your courage, and that one day that esteem may allow them to find it within themselves to do what they hold in awe of you.*

bur·den

noun

Something that is heavy, oppressive or difficult to endure.

When crushed by your own guilt because you're feeling you're not doing enough, it's easy to overlook the equally crushing **burden** *felt on the other side. No one wants to be dependant on another, to saddle their own needs on your generous back. And the more you do, the greater that weight can become. Which is why it helps to try to find even small ways to make them feel more independent, giving them a sense of control even as you stand by with a caregiver's watchful eye.*

par·a·dox

noun

A proposition or statement that seems to defy logic that may in fact be true.

Can selfishness and generosity exist at the same time? Guilt and kindness? Can you really take time for yourself as friends suggest, when you barely have time to provide the care to which you've committed? The life of the caregiver is laced with contradiction. And what may be black or white to those on the outside is not so in the world of the caregiver. You've been challenged to live within a special place where things are in conflict and oftentimes not as they seem. And while it may be difficult for others to understand, you accept the **paradox** *of the caregiver, that sea of emotional gray that out of bravery, fear or good fortune, you somehow find your way through.*

sen·try

noun

One who stands guard.

*You are a **sentry** on a mission to protect the one you love. You question the doctor. Check the prescriptions. Monitor the care when you need to surrender your charge to others. Nothing gets by you. You are a guard of body and soul, always ready to speak up, to bark if necessary, to assure that the person who so needs your fidelity, benefits from it.*

time-out

noun

A temporary break in an event or activity.

*Never underestimate the recuperative value of a **time-out**. Even compassion needs a good night's sleep. It needs time spent with friends. And an opportunity to sit on the sidelines and catch its breath. While guilt may whisper to you otherwise, caring for yourself is essential to your ability to care for another. So, take a moment, take a minute, take it now.*

right·eous

adjective

Acting in accordance with what is right,
just or equitable.

What you do can be tough, messy and sometimes so thankless that you feel like giving up. But you don't. Something inside tells you to put aside your thoughts of unfairness, and do what love demands. And you do. And that puts you on the road to one of mankind's special places, the land of the **righteous** *– a place where it's said that vast fields of good works sway in the wind, and where caregivers are welcomed with open arms.*

cra·zy

adjective

Out of control or extreme.

As if caregiving is not difficult enough, there are times when everything around you goes **crazy**, making it nearly impossible to focus on the need at hand. Murphy's Law becomes the law of your land – the weather turns against you, the traffic leaves you idling and your cell phone takes a dive. You know those days. The ones where you too, come unhinged. But there is no need to worry. You may in fact, temporarily lose your mind. But your tenacious, loving determination will ultimately restore sanity, and let you move on with your care until the next straightjacket-moment erupts.

star

noun

An object of burning gas that generates light in the night sky.

*It will never be seen by the naked eye or even with the most powerful telescope that wanders the night sky. But there will be a **star** named after you. It will be a small simple one, hiding behind better-known and more famous constellations. Diminutive but bright, it will shine of your good works. Yes - someday there will be a star named after you. Now, for lack of a better name, we'll just call it Love.*

sur·ren·der

verb

To relinquish custody or control.

There may come a time when your own compassionate proficiency is no longer enough. Greater care will be required, and you'll need to **surrender** *your loved one to the higher echelons of medicine. But don't think of it as a failure of care. Think of it as an unselfish recognition of greater need, greater than you can provide. Remember that you're not giving up, just giving over. As always, you will still be there. Same love and concern. Just a different, yet equally valuable role.*

com·mu·ni·ty

noun

A group of people with common organization
or interests.

When you're feeling alone and isolated in your caregiving, remember that you're part of a large, wondrous **community**, *an army of people doing the same good works as you, many of them feeling equally lonely in their efforts. So, take solace in knowing that when you're rendering your care, countless others are doing the same. When you're tired in body and soul, remember the equal exhaustion of your counterparts and use it as an incentive to find your second wind. The community of caregivers is always there in spirit to support you, to nudge you to try harder, to help you do the job you promised. Their strength becomes yours and in a beautiful way, yours then becomes theirs.*

ac·tor

noun

A person who plays a role in a theatrical production.

*Even if you have never stepped on stage in your entire life, caregiving demands that at times, you be a good **actor**. When they are filled with worry and concern, you need to reassure them by acting fearless. When things are going downhill fast, you need to smile broadly and glow with a positive attitude. You need to be a person of a thousand faces, a thousand different emotions, all aimed at making your audience-of-one more comfortable and thankful for the powerful supporting role you play in their personal real-life drama.*

curse

noun

Something that creates suffering or misery.

*Is caregiving a **curse** that is a blessing in disguise? If so, then most would prefer their blessings showered in another, easier way. Caregiving is simply hard work, oftentimes delivered with immense sincerity with moments of self-pity and reluctance in between. In the end, caregiving is one of life's great confrontations. Whether you face it with open arms or a clenched fist is really not the issue. Your acceptance of it is honorable enough.*

faith

noun

A conviction or belief in an idea or person.

Faith *is the line of all-you-have-to-go-by breadcrumbs you follow on the caregiver's path. Crumbs of hope that things are not as bad as they seem, and crumbs of stamina that provide the will to move on. Regardless of whether left by God, a mentor or just something deep inside of you, remember that the crumbs are your friends. Let them take you where they will.*

wal·low

verb

To act in a self-indulgent way.

Sometimes it's just delicious to **wallow** *in your over-whelming duties as a caregiver. It gives you a reason to suffer, to be a martyr for the cause. And while feeling really good about feeling really bad is an option, a better one is to graciously accept help from others when it's offered. While it may break up your emotional monopoly, both you and the one for whom you care, will be better off because of it.*

tired

adjective

Exhausted, weary or drained.

Tired *is the adjective that can modify your very being, twenty-four hours a day. Like a bag of rocks over your shoulder, caregiving weighs you down, making your efforts even more difficult to accomplish. And no – your constant weariness does not build character, nor is it its own reward. But it does exhaust any doubt of your willingness to help one you love – something that will ultimately let you sleep peacefully when better times allow.*

walk

verb

To move by putting one foot in front of the other.

*Caregiving is a **walk**-the-walk proposition. It's not about expedient thoughts and prayers sent out through social media. It's about being there. In person. Ready to help. Committed to going the distance. It's about giving up a valuable portion of your life to another. And there is nothing more valuable than that.*

per·se·ver·ance

noun

Determination, tenacity, or spunk in the face of something challenging.

Perseverance *is the never-give-up gene in your DNA. It helps you endure all-consuming days and sleepless nights. Allows you to put up with the cranky moods that can occur in the world of care. And gifts you with the patience to sit for hours in doctors' waiting rooms without being rewarded with definitive answers to vital medical questions. While everything you do may be genuinely done out of love, what actually allows you to accomplish such a feat is simply the moxie of which you are made. Find it within, and you will prevail.*

noun

An entity that lives in a lamp that grants wishes when the lamp is rubbed.

*You know there is no magic in what you do. It is just hard, challenging work that never seems to end. Yet even if unstated, you are the **genie** in the lamp to the one who looks to you. You are the answer to their most important wishes – a hand to hold, a shoulder on which to lean, the strong, undeniable sense of love that you surround them with through your care.*

tri·ath·lon

noun

A contest of three events, normally of the
athletic kind.

While you never even had a chance to train for it, you have entered the **Triathlon** *of Caregiving. First, it's swimming way over your head trying to find the time to care. Then it's running around so much that you never see your family. Finally, it's the exhausting feeling that you have no time for yourself. The Triathlon of Caregiving is a difficult race where winning is never the objective – willingness is. And your generous spirit is richly rewarded for the courage just to take it on.*

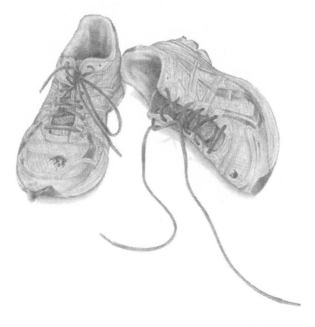

mir·a·cle

noun

An occurrence that cannot be explained by science or the laws of nature.

In devoting yourself to the care of another, a beautiful **miracle** *happens. Relieving their stress through your own care and concern can give you a sense of peace. And each pill you so conscientiously administer can also make you feel better inside. Everything you do for one in need can fill some need inside of you. And that is a miracle. Not of science, but of the healing power of the human spirit.*

worth

noun

The high caliber of personal traits that make up one's value.

You will never be paid an hourly rate for your caregiving. You will not get time and a half after eight hours, or double for working weekends. And don't expect a bonus at the end of the year. Caregiving is all hours and no rate. Of your own free will, it's giving everything you've got – your time, your love, and sometimes your own health and wellbeing. And while there is nothing monetary to weigh against the care you provide, somewhere there is a human time clock that is punched, recording every good work you do, verifying your true and inestimable **worth**.

ok

adjective

Acceptable, fitting or suitable.

*It's **ok** to be angry. Ok to feel sorry for yourself. Ok to turn your back on your caregiver title for a minute, a few hours, maybe a day. It's ok if your guilt sometimes photobombs your fragile self-image. Because you, in spite of what you may think, are very much ok.*

vo·tive

adjective

Something offered in relationship to a vow.

*You are the prayer answered to a **votive** candle lit. Perhaps they didn't know if anyone would even be aware of their request or come to their aid. But somehow that simple flame of faith found its way to you. And you responded, offering your help to someone in need. Someday, who knows when, you too may light a candle asking that someone tend to you. Trust that your prayer will be answered – the wick will still be warm and your good works will be the accelerant, the votive ready to be lit for you.*

noun

Great delight, happiness or bliss.

To the unaffected, **joy** *is as big as a parade, as loud as a rock concert, as exciting as a Florida theme park. To caregivers, joy is a much smaller matter. It's that moment when the stars align and it's all good, even if only for what seems an infinitesimal amount of time. It's the great report from the doctor that arrives the same day as a great report card from one of your kids. And to end your day on a bright note, it's the stunning, Hi-Def sunset that hits your windshield on your way home from another hard session of care. For caregivers, big joy comes in small packages. And who needs a parade anyway?*

care·giv·er

noun

A person who helps another in need.

Simple words may define **caregiver**, *but in real life so much of what you accomplish makes the word indefinable. What do you call the unexpected laugh you manage to get out of someone with nothing much to laugh about? How can you describe the thankfulness of a good day spent? And what word can possibly come to mind from the deep sense of trust developed through your time together? As a caregiver, you can only truly be defined by the generous actions you take. And those actions, large or small, are always profound. For them. For you. For everyone.*

About the Author-Caregiver

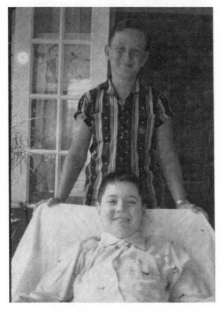

Caregiving happens. It changes you forever.

I was nine when my childhood came to an abrupt halt when my older brother, Peter, became a statistic in the polio epidemic of 1955. After a year in an iron lung he was able to come home, his breathing made possible by a portable respirator. His paralysis was total – all he could do was turn his head from left to right.

So, I became brother-caregiver. That meant feeding him, sharing his daily bedpan needs, and placing plaster casts on his arms and legs at night so his atrophied muscles wouldn't gnarl like twisted tree roots as he grew. In between those duties and under his direction, I built WWII airplane and submarine models for him from plastic kits.

In the summer of 1957 my parents decided I needed a break and sent me away to an overnight boy's camp for two weeks. Up until the day I left for it, Peter believed a miracle would happen and that he would be joining me. Instead, he died in his sleep in the middle of my second week at camp. He was thirteen.

Other than the survivor's guilt that sat next to me in my neighbor's car on the long ride home from camp, it would be many years before I could truly understand the emotions that were formed inside me as a child and are still with me today. And while I partnered with my sisters in the care of our parents before their deaths, nothing has impacted my life more than the intense experience in my youth.

Writing became therapeutic for me as a teenager and eventually provided a career in advertising, as well as an opportunity to write a daily syndicated newspaper piece and a published novel. This book is especially important to me. It's not only my way to honor caregivers, but also a way for me to participate in the community of caregivers with a story of my own, and in the process, exorcise some of the caregiving demons I have unnecessarily collected over the years.

Like most, I was not ready for the awesome task that caregiving can be. It's so easy to feel completely inadequate, to be disappointed in yourself even when doing the best you can. Fortunately, time is also a caregiver, allowing one to eventually heal – by finding joy in the good accomplished, forgiveness, even when none is in order, and life made richer by the experience.

I know writing this book has helped to heal me a bit. I hope reading it does the same for you.

CPSIA information can be obtained
at www.ICGtesting.com
Printed in the USA
LVOW08s0731201217
560362LV00006B/1977/P